POEMS AND PARAPHRASES

JAMES REEVES

Poems and Paraphrases

Quivi era men che notte e men che giorno,
Si che il viso m'andava innanzi poco;
Ma io senti' sonare un alto corno . . .

INFERNO

HEINEMANN
1972

Heinemann Educational Books Ltd
LONDON EDINBURGH MELBOURNE TORONTO
AUCKLAND SINGAPORE JOHANNESBURG
HONG KONG NAIROBI IBADAN
NEW DELHI

SBN 435 14768 4

First published 1972

Published by Heinemann Educational Books Ltd
48 Charles Street, London W1X 8AH
Designed by Ruari McLean
Printed in Great Britain by The Stellar Press Ltd
Welham Green, Hatfield, Herts

POEMS

PARAPHRASES OF FRENCH AND GERMAN POEMS

OEMS

OUGH WEATHER

o share with you this rough, divisive weather
nd not to grieve because we have to share it,
esire to wear the dark of night together
nd feel no colder that we do not wear it,
ecause sometimes my sight of you is clearer,
he memory not clouded by the sense,
o know that nothing now can make you dearer
han does the close touch of intelligence,
o be the prisoner of your kindnesses
nd tell myself I want you to be free,
o wish you here with me despite all this,
o wish you here, knowing you cannot be –
his is a way of love in our rough season,
his side of madness, the other side of reason.

THE SPARK

If, as you read, you sigh and yawn,
Remember, I am one who talks
And thinks and writes and does not live.
So if I say I live in you,
Do not retort I overstate:
I reverence him, I warm to her,
I love them but they do not feed
The fire by which I almost live.

The fire by which I almost live
Was once a blaze, is now a spark,
So if you sigh and yawn, that spark
Will brighter glow because you breathe.

NOT TO BE GREEDY

Not to be greedy for you, not to hoard you;
Not to begrudge you others to whom also
You have much to give;
Not to repine at absence, imagine neglect;
Not to be jealous, envious; still less to gorge
On the self-loving sweets of gratitude,
The masochistic bread of self-abasement,
The secret hope that you will never be free,
Despite the freedom freely exchanged between us –
All this is hard. To be an ideal
Is to be hard. To be hard is an ideal.

LATE LOVE

If of this man you know the history,
Secret and innermost, then you know well
That of the four loves of his proper being
Yours is the latest and perhaps the last.
Sounds we are born to and survive our age
Are those the wind makes, blowing round the world,
To which we add 'I want, I wish, I love'.
We give the cosmic breath significance.

SEPTEMBER DUSK

The girl and the five boys have gone with their
  burden of apples,
A tangle of bright clothes and disputation.
Darkness spreads from under the leaves of the fig-tree,
The brown nut-tree and the bramble thicket.
The territorial birds have stationed themselves
  for the night;
Some talk – none sings. There can be too much silence,
And too much certainty, as that your light tread
Will not disturb this gloom, your voice this silence.
In mockery perhaps it might be asking
'What is a thousand miles to one who hears?'
And I might answer,
  'Simplest things are hardest to accept.
Distance is simple. Causes of grief are many,
  but all simple.'
Children and birds have closed the book of day,
But I shall turn the pages of the night
Lying with my erosive enemy
Far from the echo of a voice, a footfall.

SENTIMENTAL NEW YEAR WISHES
For the Muse

I wish you what I had and lost.
I wish you what I never had.
I wish you what will hurt me most,
The good that will make good the bad.

MESSAGE

Be absolute for poetry, my friend,
Or your insatiate spirit will go hungry,
Knocking on deaf men's doors to ask for bread.
Who has the saving word will never starve.
There was a wave of bitterness on which
I swam ashore. Naked, companionless,
I had exactly life and nothing more.
The fates gave us a choice of this or that.
There is no bargaining. It was either death
Or life upon this salty element,
Banged from one desperate corner to the next,
The taste of salt for ever on my tongue.

CLOISTERED

Let us not visualise the shapes of love
Nor the demure tonality of features
But reason of the archetypal dove,
The special iconography of creatures,
So to alleviate our minds' despair
By riddling out the symbols of the air.
Pictorial brotherhoods contrive to see
The Holy Ghost as ornithology.

SONG [Suffer these hands]

Suffer these hands, the heart's interpretation.
Because I come to you as one who comes
Not at the minute's nor the mind's dictation,
Suffer these hands, the heart's interpretation.

1930

SONG [Music, they said]

Music, they said, built cities
That wore their bells like flowers;
Flowers, I thought, could heal
The hurt of savage hours.
But this was all a fiction:
It was the fact of you
That woke me from the music
Whence flowers and cities grew.

1950

YOU TOO WILL LEARN TO CRY

You too will learn to cry when you are older
And know there is no gain in holding back.
The rigid mouth, poised eyebrow and cold shoulder
Are tokens, not of fullness, but of lack.

The scalding tears of infants rolling down
Express the plenitude of sheer despair:
You realise by then that rainstorms drown
Acres of drought, and tempests cool the air.

PROUD WALKERS

See the proud walkers toss
Their curled, magnificent hair,
Vain in a world of loss
And a polluted air.

And age can give you nothing
Except a taste for death,
The sourness of self-loathing,
Truth on the final breath.

THE CHILDREN

These pretty children with their reading eyes
Distract you from the journey and the prize.
It is an innocent, a chaste distraction;
Of you they make this innocent exaction,
That you take note of them, and smile, and look,
And be at once their mirror and their book.
They need it so, and you desire it so;
And through your voice in time they come to know
The essential difference of their condition,
Demanding as their right its recognition.
The courting tone is now their expectation,
Monarch and subject each in his own station.
And if they harden, they will feel no shame;
For their corruption you must take the blame.
Their watching eyes will read, as due, your guilt,
On which, and not on their mere pride, is built
The boundless bounty of their self-regard.
Necessities of self-defence are hard.
Pursue the journey; suffer to be wise,
And win the loser's consolation prize.

FIN DE SAISON

Much of my life – how much? – has been transacted
At café counters on the sunny streets:
But now evening descends, the leaves descend,
And yawning waiters hurry on my death.
It is ordained no man shall have for long
The faculty of self-regeneration,
So with a syllable of leave-taking,
A final tip, I drift into the night.
Next week the cafés close for renovation.

ANIMULA

No one knows, no one cares –
An old soul
In a narrow cottage,
A parlour,
A kitchen,
And upstairs
A narrow bedroom,
A narrow bed –
A particle of immemorial life.

A QUESTION

Adrift in the polluted garden, ask:
The uninhibiting draught, the hands' entreaty,
The night's avowal and the morning's penance –
Is there no different course, no other sequence?

MOMENTS IN HELL
[from Dante's *Inferno*]

O blind cupidity, evil and foolish,
Which in this short life is our great incentive
And proves our ruin in the life to come . . .

Help me, good Vulcan, help your master, Jove,
In Mongibello at the black forge crying.

Here there was less than night and less than day,
So that my vision went not far before,
But in my ears I felt a high horn sounding.

This I have spoken so that thou mayst suffer.

I, Master Adam, coiner when alive,
Had everything I might desire, and now
Sighing I crave a single drop of water.

BAGATELLES

WHEN TWO

When two have no nutrition but the air
Love is the product of a twin despair.

EUPHORIA

The exaltation of the evening comes
When to their graves the tired members fall.
Is there no stratagem by which to save
This mood of exaltation for us all?

TO HELP US

Technology has found no way
To help us, in our desperation,
Build on the ruin of a day
An evening's reconciliation.

IN LESS THAN SECONDS

I look into their beautiful passing faces.
In less than seconds worlds have swum apart.

ROBERTO GERHARD'S FOURTH SYMPHONY

A strong noise hits the amber air,
The ambient air about my chair;
By which I know there is an affirmation
Of what you might call neo-civilisation.

A VOICE

How badly and how beautifully she speaks.
Her voice is like a Sunday evening chime,
As stupid and evocative as her face,
Moving and childish as an ancient rhyme.

A MYSTERY

Some necessary jottings of my trade
I noted lately on a tape-recorder
Today, a fortnight after, when replayed
Revealed a message of a different order . . .

ONE PROPRIETY

There's only one propriety
(Whatever you may think) –
To nurture in sobriety
The brats we get in drink.

ACT OF MERCY

The deaf, blind cripple shuffled on,
Was cornered by the corner-lurkers,
Gave no resistance, groaned and died –
And cheated all the welfare-workers.

VARIATION ON A CLICHÉ

She stood you up, she let you down,
She smashed your pride, the red red rose;
So now in disarray you stand,
A carving knife in your right hand
And in your left a severed nose.

ETHOLOGY

When the geese write a book
On Konrad Lorenz,
Ethology
Will begin to make sense.

PARAPHRASES
OF FRENCH AND GERMAN POEMS

SPLEEN

[after *Spleen* by Charles Baudelaire]

I am the prince of a rain-sodden kingdom,
Rich and yet powerless, young and very old;
The curtseys of my mentors I disdain,
And pass the time in boredom with my dogs,
In hunting and in hawking take no pleasure
Nor in my people starving at the gates.
The drollest ballad of my favourite jester
Excites no laughter in this harsh, sick prince.
My bed, powdered with lilies, is a tomb.
The ladies of the chamber think me handsome
But can contrive no costume so indecent
As to regale this youthful skeleton.
The man of science with his potable gold
Has never purged my body of corruption,
And in those blood-baths we derive from Rome,
Remembered in old age by men of power,
I have not learned to warm my sluggish corpse.
Where green Lethean water flows, not blood.

TWILIGHT

[after *Le Crépuscule du Soir*
by Charles Baudelaire]

See where delightful evening, friend of the crook,
Partner in crime, comes with his wolf tread.
Like a huge alcove slowly the sky shuts.
Men cannot wait to change into wild beasts.

Evening, dear evening, haven of him whose arms
Can truly tell him 'We have worked today',
Of him whose heart is crushed by savage grief,
The dogged scholar with the brow of lead
And the bowed labourer trudging home to sleep.
Meanwhile the unwholesome demons of the air
Wake heavily like business men, take wing
And bang themselves on gables and on shutters.
Then gaudy prostitution in the streets
Begins to flaunt beneath the flapping lights,
Issues from ant-hill apertures, marks out
Ubiquitous secret tracks, as one who plots
A sudden ambush. Like a ravening worm
It gnaws the breast of the polluted city.

You hear on every side the hiss of kitchens,
The squeaking theatres and snorting bands,
Those gambling-hells, the sleezy restaurants
Fill up with tarts and their accomplice sharks.
Thieves too, who work without respite or pity,
Pry open doors and safes with gentle fingers,
To eat for a few days and trick out their whores.

At this climactic hour let me withdraw
And still the clamour. Is it not the time
That sharpens all the anguish of the sick?
The stranglehold of night is on their necks.
They near their journey's end and move towards
The common pit; their sighing fills the poorhouse.
Some never more at dusk will know again
The chimney corner and the fragrant soup
Beside a loved companion. All their lives
Some have not known the warmth and tenderness
Of their own fireside. They have never lived.

HARMONIES OF EVENING

[after *Harmonie du Soir* by Charles Baudelaire]

These are the moments when on vibrant stems
The flowers yield up their being like a censer.
Perfumes and sounds eddy upon the air
– A melancholy dance, a whirling languor.

The flowers yield up their being like a censer.
The violin shudders like a heart in torment
– A melancholy dance, a whirling languor.
The sky's sad beauty is a pilgrim's rest.

The violin shudders like a heart in torment,
A tender heart hating the black abyss.
The sky's sad beauty is a pilgrim's rest.
In its own stiffening blood the sun is drowned.

A tender heart hating the black abyss
Gathers all remnants of the luminous past.
In its own stiffening blood the sun is drowned.
Your memory glows within me like a chalice.

THE ALBATROSS

[after *L'Albatros* by Charles Baudelaire]

Sometimes the idle seamen take
That huge seabird the albatross
Who, indolent fellow-voyager,
Pursues them in their salty wake.

This king who in the blue sky soars
Is lowered level with the deck.
There, shamefaced, clumsy, pitiable,
He trails his grand white wings like oars.

A sailor mocks his limping gait
Or offers him a pipe to smoke.
The winged sky-wanderer, crippled now,
Has lost all dignity and state.

The poet in his cloud-dominions
Laughs at the fowler, rides the storm;
On earth amidst the jeers of men
Is maimed by his own giant pinions.

SIR PERCIVALE
[after *Parsifal* by Paul Verlaine]

Sir Percivale has overcome the girls,
Their pleasant chatter and diverting lust;
Has overcome his virgin boy's desire
For their small breasts and their diverting chatter,
Has overcome the subtle-hearted beauty
Displaying her cool arms and sensual throat,
Has conquered Hell, returning to his tent
His boy's arm weighted with a heavy trophy,
That spear with which the sacred flank was pierced;
He has healed the King: now he is King himself,
Priest of the quintessential, holiest treasure;
As glory and symbol, in a golden robe,
Adores the chalice with the real blood –
And O those children chanting in the choir!

HUNTING HORNS

[after *Cors de Chasse* by Guillaume Apollinaire]

Noble and tragic as a tyrant's mask,
Our story has no drama and no peril.
No trivial touch lends pathos to our love.

Thomas de Quincey went to his poor Anne
In dreams of opium, poison sweet and chaste;
And since all passes, let us too pass by.
Let us pass by – but I shall turn again.

Our memories, are they not hunting horns,
Their resonances dying on the wind?

ALIENATION

[after *Vereinsamt* by Friedrich Nietsche]

Townwards on skirring wing
Now flies the raucous crow.
He has a home, and it is well with him;
Soon it will snow.

Stiff now you stand,
Backward your lingering gaze.
Fool – to have fled into the winter world
Before the bitter days.

The world that is a gate
Into a thousand waste-lands mute and cold
For one who has lost all you have lost
No resting-place can hold.

Now fated to a winter quest you stand
With terror in your eyes.
You are like smoke
For ever seeking colder skies.

Fly bird; grate out your song
With vulture voice.
Fool – let your bloody heart be hidden
By scorn and ice.

Townwards on skirring wing
Now flies the raucous crow;
Wretched is he who has no home –
Soon it will snow.

THE OFFICE DESK

[after *Aktentisch* by Theodor von Storm]

Today I signed directives at the office
And almost felt the common man's temptation
Of saying to myself 'A good day's work',
Deriving thence a stupid, small elation.

THE TWO

[after *Die Beiden* by Hugo von Hofmannsthal]

Like the full wine-cup in her hand
Her smiling mouth was round;
Her steadfast tread was light and sure,
No drop spilled on the ground.

The horse that carried him was young;
As firm as hers the hand
That with a careless movement made
His horse beside her stand.

But when he reached to take the cup,
Their fingers trembled so,
They saw between them on the ground
The red wine darkly flow.

WORLD'S END
[after *Weltende* by Jakob van Hoddis]

The hat flies off the bourgeois' pointed head.
The air is torn by screams on every side.
Slaters fall off the roofs and break in half.
On all sea coasts, we read, fast flows the tide.

Fast flows the tide. The tempest has arrived.
The wild waves hop ashore. The dams are crumbling.
Most of mankind are suffering from colds,
And from the bridges railway trains are tumbling.

POEM

[after *Gedicht* by Gottfried Benn]

And what do these compulsions mean,
Part word, part image and part notion?
From what internal pressure comes
This quiet, sorrowing emotion?

Impressions flow from nothingness,
From single things and from a heap.
One yields a flame, another ashes.
You scatter them, and quench, and keep.

Set frontiers, then, about some things:
You know you cannot grasp the whole.
Beneath the spell of vague misgivings
You will remain thus in control.

You shape and hammer and engrave
All day, all night, and Sundays too.
The vessel is of finished silver,
And it is being. It is you.

A DECLARATION OF LOVE

[after *Ein Liebes Bekenntnis* by Max Herrmann-Neisse]

To me your absence is like death;
My presence is like death to you.
I fail you: how can you forgive?
We kiss at parting – then alone we live.

And then alone you see my love.
In such a love where is the truth?
What use my sad and searching gaze
When never a spoken word my love betrays?

Once more you leave me here alone
Lost in a helpless agony
Which drives me out into the night . . .
My one desire to have you in my sight.

I hear the laughter in the houses;
I see the couples hurrying home
As if on wings, their arms entwined.
An envious fever suffocates my mind.

But if we were together now
Your eyes would not be on my book;
Shut and forbidding, I would see
Your loved face vainly beg one word from me.

So I demand perpetual pardon.
In debt to you until the end
I am your child: you gave me breath
And I require your blessing at my death.

AUTUMN TRANSFIGURED

[after *Verklärte Herbst* by Georg Trakl]

The closing year explodes
In golden wine and fruit;
The hushed woods standing round
Befriend the lonely man.

The labourer approves;
Birds greet him as he goes.
The soft, slow chimes of dusk
Give courage for the end.

It is love's gentle hour;
Image is one with image.
The blue stream bears the boat
In calm and silence down.

HE PLUM TREE

fter *Der Pflaumenbaum* by Bertold Brecht]

puny tree grows in our yard –
plum you'd hardly call it.
bout this tree a paling stands
n case some harm befall it.

can't grow big, though any tree
Vould like the chance to sprout;
ut that can never happen here:
he sun is quite shut out.

ou wouldn't know it was a plum;
t's never borne a fruit.
et you can tell what tree it is
n spring when green leaves shoot.